The Nez Perce

by Petra Press

Content Adviser: Dr. Bruce Bernstein, Assistant Director for Cultural Resources, National Museum of the American Indian, Smithsonian Institution

Social Science Adviser: Professor Sherry L. Field, Department of Curriculum and Instruction, College of Education, The University of Texas at Austin

Reading Adviser: Dr. Linda D. Labbo, Department of Reading Education, College of Education, The University of Georgia

COMPASS POINT BOOKS

Minneapolis, Minnesota

Compass Point Books
3722 West 50th Street, #115
Minneapolis, MN 55410

Visit Compass Point Books on the Internet at *www.compasspointbooks.com* or e-mail your request
to *custserv@compasspointbooks.com*

Cover: An Appaloosa horse wearing a beaded Nez Perce saddle

Photographs ©: Marilyn "Angel" Wynn, cover, 4, 7, 14, 15, 18–19, 21, 22, 23, 24–25, 26, 28–29,
35, 39, 40, 41, 42–43; University of Washington, 8-9; D. Wilder/Tom Stack & Associates, 10; Eda
Rogers, 11; North Wind Picture Archives, 12–13; Thomas Kitchin/Tom Stack & Associates, 16;
Corbis, 17; Bettmann/Corbis, 30; Denver Public Library/Western History Department, 31, 36;
Oregon Trail Museum Association, 32–33; Stock Montage, 34; National Portrait Gallery,
Smithsonian Institution/Art Resource, NY, 37.

Editors: E. Russell Primm, Emily J. Dolbear, and Alice K. Flanagan
Photo Researchers: Svetlana Zhurkina and Jo Miller
Photo Selector: Catherine Neitge
Designer: Bradfordesign, Inc.
Cartographer: XNR Productions, Inc.

Library of Congress Cataloging-in-Publication Data
Press, Petra.
   The Nez Perce / by Petra Press.
     p. cm. — (First reports)
   Includes bibliographical references and index.
   ISBN 0-7565-0187-3
   1. Nez Perce Indians—Juvenile literature. 2. Nez Percé Indians. [1. Indians of North America—
Northwest Pacific.] I. Title. II. Series.
E99.N5 P74 2002
979.5004'9741—dc21   2001004414

Table of Contents

▲ A Nez Perce dancer

People of the Plateau

For thousands of years the Nez Perce (pronounced nehz PURS) have lived in the northwestern United States. These Native Americans lived on the high, flat land between the Cascade Mountains and the Rocky Mountains.

The Nez Perce built their villages along the Snake, Clearwater, and Salmon Rivers. They hunted buffalo and fished for salmon. They lived off of the land.

The **plateau** where the Nez Perce lived has grassy flatlands and rolling hills. People often call the Nez Perce the "Plateau Indians."

Nez Perce is a French term that means "pierced nose." This name came from a French trapper who saw some Nez Perce people wearing shells in their noses.

The Nez Perce call themselves *Nimi'ipu*. This word means the "real people" or "we the people."

The Nez Perce homelands and reservations

▲ *A tepee marks the burial memorial of Old Chief Joseph in the Wallowa Valley in Oregon, homeland of the Nez Perce.*

Today, most of the Nez Perce live on or near **reservations**. These reservations are in Idaho, Oregon, and the state of Washington.

Summer and Winter Homes

In the past, the Nez Perce moved their villages when the seasons changed. A village usually included five or six houses. Sometimes, several villages joined together to form **bands**.

The Nez Perce built different houses for warm and cold weather. The houses for warm weather were easy to put up and take down. They could be moved quickly. In spring and summer, they set up camp near the mountains, where it was cooler.

In warm weather they built long rectangular houses called long-houses. A longhouse was made of wooden poles. It was covered with woven plants or buffalo skins.

Sometimes, thirty families lived in one longhouse. Each family had its own living area and fireplace.

◄ *A longhouse from the late nineteenth century*

In winter, the Nez Perce set up villages in the canyons along the Columbia and Snake Rivers. The canyon walls protected them from the wind.

▲ *The Nez Perce lived in canyons along the Snake River.*

In winter, the Nez Perce lived in small pit houses. They dug the floors deep into the ground. They covered the roofs with cedar bark and plants. People climbed into the house through a hole in the roof.

Later, when the Nez Perce began to hunt buffalo on horseback, they lived in tepees. A tepee was a cone-shaped tent that was easy to move.

Today, the Nez Perce live in modern homes. But many still use tepees during festivals.

▲ *The Nez Perce hunted buffalo.*

Food

The rivers provided much food for the Nez Perce. About 80 percent of their food was fish. They ate lots

of salmon. Each spring and fall, millions of salmon swam upstream from the Pacific Ocean.

The Nez Perce caught fish in many ways. Men speared fish. They also used nets, small traps, or hooks. Some people even used clubs and bows and arrows to catch fish.

The Nez Perce ate the fish they caught. They also dried the fish in the sun or over a smoky fire. These fish were stored for the Nez Perce to eat in the winter.

◄ Native Americans caught salmon in the Columbia River.

▲ *Tools were used to dig roots and bulbs.*

Other food came from the ground. The women gathered berries, wild onions, carrots, nuts, grasses, and herbs.

In late June and July, a wild lily called camas (pronounced KA-mus) was in bloom. The camas bulb looks like an onion but tastes sweet.

▲ *Tepees are pitched at the edge of a camas field.*

Each summer, people from many villages gathered at the camas grounds for weeks at a time. The women and girls dug up bulbs. The men and boys hunted and played games. It was a favorite time for bands to get to know one another.

▲ Elk have been an important food source for the Nez Perce for generations.

▲ *A Nez Perce chief on horseback in 1877*

The food that was most difficult for the Nez Perce to get was meat. Before they rode horses, the Nez Perce hunted on foot. They looked for deer, elk, bear, and mountain goats. They often walked for days and returned with nothing.

With horses, the Nez Perce hunters could travel much faster. They could also carry more of what they caught on horseback. The Nez Perce still eat deer, elk, and salmon.

Family and Community

The Nez Perce were loyal to their family and community. They also believed that everyone had a right to

Nez Perce tribal members gather for a celebration.

make his or her own decisions. Even warriors could decide if they wanted to fight.

An older man usually served as the village chief. He looked after the village members. But he could not tell the people what to do.

The largest village in a band had a leader, a peace chief, and a war chief. Band leaders and important warriors were on the village **council**. They made big decisions, such as when to go to war or where to move the village.

Today, the Nez Perce people still have a council. They elect nine people to handle the business of the tribe.

Today, as in the past, villages hold open council meetings. Everyone has a say. Women have always been included in tribal decisions.

A Nez Perce woman could choose her husband. She lived with her husband's family. She could disagree with her husband or other tribal members, however. Her opinions were respected.

▲ The Nez Perce have always respected women's opinions.

▲ *A statue shows a Nez Perce woman and girl digging for camas bulbs.*

A Nez Perce family included aunts, uncles, and grandparents. Children worked and played with their relatives. They learned important lessons and skills that way.

Boys hunted, fished, and made tools. They learned how to behave as fathers, husbands, hunters, and warriors.

Girls gathered, cooked, and preserved food. They also made clothing. They learned how to behave as mothers, wives, and village keepers.

▲ *A Nez Perce man plays a traditional flute.*

The older tribal members were well respected. They were the teachers and the storytellers. Through stories, they continue to pass the tribe's history and beliefs down to the younger members.

Religion

The Nez Perce have always lived close to nature. They believed that spirits lived in animals and plants. There were spirits in the water, earth, and sky.

Some spirits were evil. Others played tricks on hu-

mans. One trickster called Coyote kept the world safe from evil spirits. But he also got into a lot of trouble.

The Nez Perce respect one Great Spirit above all others. His name is *Hanyawat* (Old One). The people believe that he created life and all the spirits in it.

The Nez Perce held ceremonies to thank the spirits. They also honored the spirits of the dead.

Shamans led these ceremonies. Men and women were shamans. They sang and offered herb medicines.

In their early teen years, boys and girls went on a **vision quest**. They spent several days alone in the hills. They **fasted** and prayed.

◄ *The director of the Nez Perce Wolf Education and Research Center in Winchester, Idaho, plays a flute to the wolves every morning.*

▲ *A Nez Perce shaman holds an eagle staff.*

They asked for a spirit to come to them in a vision. This spirit was called a **wyakin**. This spirit would protect and guide them the rest of their lives.

Explorers and Traders

In the mid 1700s, trappers from Canada and the American colonies arrived in Nez Perce territory. They came to trap beaver. Beaver hats and coats were popular at the time in Europe and America.

The Nez Perce had few beaver furs, but they had horses. The Nez Perce had gotten horses in the early 1700s. They quickly became skilled at breeding and training horses. These strong horses were called Appaloosas. The trappers wanted the Nez Perce horses.

The Nez Perce welcomed the trappers. They traded their horses for metal knives, cooking tools, and woolen blankets. Slowly, however, the friendly relationship changed.

In the late 1700s, the American colonies won independence from Britain. Soon, American settlers began moving west into Indian homelands.

In 1804, U.S. president Thomas Jefferson sent Meriwether Lewis and William Clark to explore land in the Northwest. Their famous trip lasted more than two years and covered 8,000 miles (12,872 kilometers). By the 1840s, thousands of settlers were traveling the Oregon Trail into Nez Perce country.

◄ *A statue of explorers Lewis and Clark meeting the Nez Perce*

Guns and Promises

The traders and settlers who came west brought guns. Guns changed the peaceful way people lived.

For protection, the Nez Perce got guns, too. In time, they became expert shooters.

In 1855, the Nez Perce joined other tribes in Walla Walla (Washington Territory). They met with U.S. leaders to discuss sharing the land.

▲ *The Nez Perce met with government leaders and other tribes at Walla Walla in 1855.*

After several days, the Native Americans agreed to sign a **treaty**—the Nez Perce Treaty of 1855. In the treaty, the U.S. government promised to build houses, hospitals, and schools for the Indians. It also promised food, animals, and farming supplies.

In return, the Indians would give up their land and move to reservations. The U.S. government promised that the land would be theirs forever. The U.S. government did not keep its promises.

▲ *Nez Perce students at a school in Oregon in the late nineteenth century*

Broken Treaties and War

In 1863, gold was discovered on the Nez Perce reservation. Miners, traders, and settlers rushed in. The Americans broke the Nez Perce treaty. Soon they

began stealing Nez Perce animals and building homes on Nez Perce land.

The U.S. government did little to stop them. In fact, they forced Nez Perce leaders to give up their land in the Treaty of 1863.

This painting by artist William Henry Jackson shows settlers heading west along the Oregon Trail.

In 1877, the U.S. government ordered the Nez Perce to move to a reservation in Idaho Territory. Some Nez Perce bands and Nez Perce chief Joseph refused. They did not want to leave their homeland.

Some settlers and Nez Perce began fighting. It turned into a war. The Nez Perce did not want to fight the U.S. Army and tried to escape to Canada.

Over the next three months, more than 700 Nez Perce traveled

▲ *Chief Joseph would not leave his homeland.*

across Idaho, Wyoming, and Montana. White settlers were alarmed by so many Indians moving across the country.

Three armies chased the Nez Perce. Several times soldiers caught up with them. But each time, the Nez Perce outsmarted the army.

▲ *The Big Hole National Battlefield in Montana is the site of an August 1877 fight between the Nez Perce and U.S. troops.*

The Nez Perce never attacked any white settlements. At one town, they even bought supplies with gold dust and cash.

By October, the Nez Perce were low on supplies. Many families were sick and tired. They stopped to rest less than 40 miles (64 kilometers) from the Canadian border. As they rested, the army surrounded them.

▲ U.S. troops charged a Nez Perce tepee camp near the end of the War of 1877.

Chief Joseph was a great leader.

The Nez Perce fought the U.S. soldiers for five days. They were outnumbered. On October 5, 1877, the Nez Perce people gave up.

The leader of the Nez Perce, Chief Joseph, gave a powerful speech. He spoke to the warriors. "Hear me, my chiefs," Chief Joseph said. "I am tired. My heart is sick and sad. From where the sun now stands, I will fight no more forever."

Beginning Again

After the war, the Nez Perce were put in prison in Kansas. Then they went to Indian Territory in Oklahoma. Finally, they were moved to the Colville Reservation in Washington. It was a terrible time for the Nez Perce.

Chief Joseph showed his greatness, however. He spoke for his people. He asked for fair treatment for the tribe. He asked President Theodore Roosevelt to let the Nez Perce return to their homeland, but he was refused.

Chief Joseph never saw the Wallowa Valley again. He died on the Colville Reservation in 1904.

The Nez Perce suffered on the reservations. Housing and health care were poor. Food was limited. The way of life that once kept them strong was gone.

Children were sent away to boarding schools for

▲ Late nineteenth century missionary Kate McBeth poses with Nez Perce women.

years at a time. They had to speak a new language and accept new beliefs.

Native Americans could not govern themselves until Congress passed the Indian Reorganization Act of 1934. Then they were free to rule themselves.

Looking Toward the Future

▲ *Today, most Nez Perce live in Idaho, Oregon, and Washington.*

Long ago, the Nez Perce were a large and powerful tribe in the northwestern United States. Today, they own fewer than 100,000 acres (40,500 hectares) of land. In 1959, the U.S. government paid the Nez Perce nearly $20 million for their lost land. Today, the Nez Perce population numbers about 4,000. About two-thirds of the people live on or near reservations in Idaho, Washington, and Oregon.

The Nez Perce have lost much through history. But they also have shown strength and courage.

The tribe has new businesses to improve life for its people. They include horse-breeding, timber, and gambling.

▲ *The Nez Perce have set up successful businesses working with horses.*

The Nez Perce dance at a tribal gathering.

Many adults have left the reservation to find work. They work in logging camps and sawmills. Others fish on rivers in the area. Some are lawyers, teachers, and businesspeople. Some earn livings by renting out their reservation land.

The Nez Perce also understand the importance of education. The tribe is trying to improve its schools for its children. Through education, they will build a better future for their people.

The Nez Perce are proud of their history and traditions. They are also proud to be American.

Glossary

bands—groups of people who live and travel together

council—a group of people chosen to make important decisions

fasted—went without food

plateau—a high, flat land

reservations—large areas of land set aside for Native Americans; in Canada, reservations are called reserves

shamans—leaders of ceremonies to heal people or honor the spirits of the dead

treaty—an agreement between two governments

vision quest—a journey of prayer and fasting

wyakin—a spirit that protects and guides a person throughout life

Did You Know?

- The Nez Perce helped Lewis and Clark prepare for their trip west. They gave them maps of the land, food, and other supplies. In return, William Clark gave some of the Nez Perce bronze medals and U.S. flags.

- The French write *Nez Perce* with an accent mark over the last é—Nez Percé. They pronounce it nay per-SAY.

- The Nez Perce traded far and wide. They traded with Canadian Indians. They also traded with Plains Indians as far east as the Rockies and desert people as far south as California.

At a Glance

Tribal name: Nimi'ipu, meaning the "real people" or "we the people"

Past locations: Idaho, Washington, Oregon

Present locations: Idaho, Washington, Oregon

Traditional houses: Longhouses, pit houses, tepees

Traditional clothing material: Woven fiber, skins

Traditional transportation: Horses, snowshoes, wooden dugout canoes

Traditional food: Roots, wild plants, fish, meat

Important Dates

7500 B.C. Early Nez Perce settle on plateau in Idaho, Washington, and Oregon.

A.D. 1700s First white trappers visit Nez Perce lands.

1804 Lewis and Clark lead a group of explorers into Nez Perce territory.

1830s Christians set up missions to convert the Nez Perce.

1840s Settlers push west along the Oregon Trail.

1855 The Nez Perce Treaty of 1855 opens a large part of Nez Perce land to white settlers.

1863 Gold is discovered on Nez Perce land.

1874 The Nez Perce refuse to move to a reservation in Idaho.

1877 Chief Joseph leads followers to Canada to escape the U.S. Army. After several battles, he gives up. The Nez Perce are sent to North Dakota, then Kansas, and later Oklahoma.

1934 Congress passes the Indian Reorganization Act, which gives Native Americans the right to govern themselves.

1959 The Indian Claims Commission pays the Nez Perce nearly $20 million for lost land.

Want to Know More?

At the Library

Lassieur, Allison. *The Nez Perce Tribe*. Mankato, Minn.: Bridgestone Books, 2000.

Rifkin, Mark. *The Nez Perce Indians*. New York: Chelsea House, 1994.

Sanford, William R. *Chief Joseph, Nez Perce Warrior*. Springfield, N.J.: Enslow Publishers, 1994.

On the Web

The Nez Perce Tribe
http://www.nezperce.org
For the official Nez Perce Tribe web site

The Nez Perce Indians
http://www.pbs.org/lewisandclark/native/nez.html
For more information about Nez Perce history and customs

Through the Mail

Big Hole National Battlefield
P.O. Box 237
Wisdom, MT 59761
To learn about the history of the battle

On the Road

Nez Perce National Historical Park
Route 1 Box 100
Spalding, ID 83540-9715
208/843-2261
To visit the thirty-eight sites reflecting the history of the Nez Perce

About the Author

Petra Press is a freelance writer of young adult nonfiction, specializing in the diverse culture of the Americas. Her more than twenty books include histories of U.S. immigration, education, and settlement of the West, as well as portraits of numerous indigenous cultures. She lives with her husband, David, in Milwaukee, Wisconsin.